Grammar and Writing Handbook

Grade 4

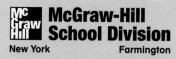

McGraw-Hill
School Division

New York   Farmington

McGraw-Hill School Division

A Division of The **McGraw·Hill** Companies

Copyright © McGraw-Hill School Division, a Division of the Educational and Professional Publishing Group of The McGraw-Hill Companies, Inc.

All rights reserved. No part of this book may be reproduced or transmitted in any form or by any means, electronic or mechanical, including photo-copying, recording, or by any information storage and retrieval system, without permission in writing from the publisher.

Editorial Development: Hudson Publishing Associates

McGraw-Hill School Division
Two Penn Plaza
New York, New York 10121

Printed in the United States of America.

ISBN 0-02-244876-4 / 4

6 7 8 9 079 04 03 02 01

TABLE OF CONTENTS

PART ONE

Writing

CONTENTS

THE WRITING PROCESS

How many ways can you exercise? You probably have fun jumping rope or running around at recess. Maybe you walk back and forth to school each day, play on a baseball team, or take dance lessons. Have you ever thought that writing is exercise, too? And it exercises more than just your fingers. Follow the steps in the writing process and find out how. Are you ready for a workout?

Prewriting

Exercise your senses! What have you seen or heard or touched that has started you thinking? Would it make a good idea for writing? As you plan what to write, explore your idea a little more. Read about it, ask questions, observe, and listen. Exercise your memory, too. What experiences or thoughts do you remember that you want to pass on to your readers? Jot down your notes and ideas.

Drafting

Exercise your communication ability! Express your ideas and thoughts on paper. Write as much as you can. Don't worry about getting everything perfect right now. It's just time to say what you want to say. Read over what you have written, and think about it. It may give you more ideas about what to include when you write more.

Revising

Exercise your skills! Now that you have your thoughts and information on paper, take a good look at your writing. Do your ideas make sense in the order you wrote them? You may wish to rearrange or even rewrite certain parts. A writing partner may give you an idea you hadn't thought of or see something that you missed.

Proofreading

When you *proofread*, check for mistakes in spelling, grammar, and punctuation. Proofreading helps to make the meaning of your writing perfectly clear.

Publishing

Exercise your imagination! How will you present your final product? Will you share your work with a family member, enter it in a contest, or display it at school? An imaginative cover, neat writing, and colorful artwork can make others want to read what you have written. Take time to look over your final work. What do you like about it? What would you do differently the next time? And remember—keep writing! After all, exercising makes you strong!

PREWRITING

keep in mind

You may want to use a chart to organize your information. You can also organize details in a:

▶ *list*
▶ *word cluster or web*
▶ *outline*
▶ *diagram*
▶ *table*
▶ *graph*
▶ *story map*

Thinking About Purpose and Audience

Perhaps you and your brother or sister want to start your own lawn care service and need to advertise it. This is called your *purpose.* Your advertisement also needs readers, or an *audience.* Your audience might be the people in your neighborhood.

Choosing a Topic and Organizing Ideas

Brainstorm on your own or with a classmate to collect ideas for your topic. Make a list. Then choose the topic you are most interested in exploring.

Make a writing plan. Use a *graphic organizer* or an outline to record your thoughts in a logical way.

Research and Inquiry

Collect as much information as you can. There are many ways to do this that will fit your topic.

▶ Ask yourself what you need to know. Talk with a friend or grownup about the kinds of facts and details you should include. Picture in your mind different things you want to present.

▶ Do the footwork! Research your idea in books and magazines at the library. Find new information and pictures on the Internet. Arrange to interview an expert about your topic. Take a field trip.

PSST!

You may need to narrow your original topic. Focus on the ideas that you think will be most useful to your readers.

DRAFTING

Writing a draft can give you a great feeling. As your first version takes shape, you begin to have a hint of what your finished product will look like. You've done your best to get ready. Now it's time to take off.

▶ Assemble the notes and information you gathered.

▶ Keep your audience and purpose in mind.

▶ Use details to create a picture in the reader's mind.

Freewriting

For now, set your mind and your pencil free. Write as much as you can. When you revise your work, you will be glad you have many ideas to work with. Put the notes from your research and the ideas from your graphic organizers into whole sentences. Now is the time to express everything you want to say about your topic.

Don't Worry!

When you are composing your rough draft, it is OK to include a word that you do not know how to spell. There will be time later to correct your spelling and make changes. When you write your rough draft, show the reader the real you.

keep in mind

Try things out first.
▶ *Think of different ways to state what you want to say.*
▶ *Ask a friend which beginning is most interesting.*
▶ *Finally, plan how you want your work to end.*

REVISING AND PROOFREADING

Think of your rough draft as an invention in progress. All the parts are there, but you find that your invention will work better if it is put together a little differently. This is called *revising*. After you finish revising, take a break! Then reread your writing. Ask yourself these questions:

▶ Do my sentences make sense? Are they arranged in a logical order?

▶ Is something missing? Do I need to elaborate?

When you *proofread*, you polish up your spelling and grammar to eliminate mistakes. You ask:

▶ Have I checked my spelling, punctuation, and grammar? Have I used the right verb tenses?

Are you tired of pulling out weeds? Are you afraid your flowers will wilt when you are away on vacation? For the anser to your problems, call Matt or Anna at:

Yes, We Can! Yard
~~Matt and Anna's Lawn~~ Care
712-4324

We can rake leaves in the fall. We work hard and our prices are reasonable. We can plant flowers in the spring, we can pull weeds and watr your flowers in the summer. You can count on us!

PUBLISHING

Publishing is the way you present your finished product to others. Whether you publish a three-page science report or send a letter to the editor of your school paper, you can show pride in what you have written. Your final copy can be handwritten or typed. Either way, it should be neat and easy to read.

Presenting

You are an author whether you present a poem to one friend or submit it to a magazine. Something you write can also be turned into a spoken presentation, like a play or a speech. Be prepared when you present. Practice what you want to say. You can use note cards to write your information in the order you want to present it.

Here are some other tips you can use when you present or when others present to you.

keep in mind

Self-Check: Reflecting is like giving your writing a checkup. Think about your finished product one more time. Identify ways you could still improve your skills. Look for ways that you did accomplish your purpose.

Listening and Speaking

▶ Listen for a speaker's main ideas. What words or phrases stand out in your mind?

▶ Is the audience formal or informal? Match the speaking style to the audinece.

Viewing and Representing

▶ If there are pictures or charts, look for details that the speaker does not mention.

▶ Make presentations clearer and more interesting by adding visuals. A large poster helps get ideas across.

TYPES OF WRITING

PERSONAL NARRATIVE

A *personal narrative* is a true story about something you have experienced. Is it a special place that makes you feel happy? A visit to someone who lives far away? What was funny, sad, or exciting?

Think, Remember, and Reflect

This type of writing helps you reflect—to look back and recall an experience in detail. What do you remember most? What was special or unique about a person or place?

A personal narrative comes to life when you express feelings in your own style. Use colorful description to help readers see and feel things exactly as you did. No one can tell your story as well as you!

Make a Plan

A good personal narrative has an *order* to help readers follow the events.

▶ Get your audience's attention with a strong beginning.

▶ Plan a beginning, middle, and end to your story.

▶ Use time-order words such as *first, next, afterwards,* and *finally.*

EXPLANATORY WRITING

Do you want to teach someone how to play a game? To take care of a pet? To make an art project? Writing that explains rules or gives instructions is called *explanatory writing*. Sometimes it is called "how-to" writing. It lists the materials, equipment, or ingredients you need, and then gives each step.

▶ Make it easy for readers to follow your steps. List them by number.

▶ Use time-order words that tell when to do each step.

▶ Give space-order details for size, shape, color, and position.

▶ Give clear details so the reader can "see" each step.

▶ Drawings or diagrams can show readers if they are on the right track.

keep in mind

Time-order words like these can help your reader follow directions:

▶ *first*

▶ *next*

▶ *then*

▶ *last* or *finally*

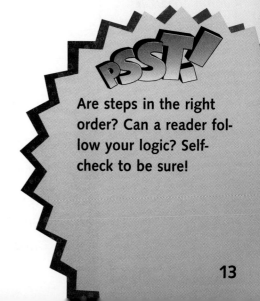

Are steps in the right order? Can a reader follow your logic? Self-check to be sure!

PERSUASIVE WRITING

Junior:	Mom, can I have new skates?
Mom:	No.
Junior:	Everybody else has new ones.
Mom:	No!
Junior:	But, mine are all scratched.
Mom:	NO!
Junior:	I'll pay half the price.
Mom:	I'll think about it.

How persuasive can you be? You may be an expert at influencing others. Persuasive writing tries to do the same thing—to persuade someone to take a certain action or think a certain way.

The Rules of the Game

We are bombarded every day with messages that try to persuade us. It is important to think about them and make the best decisions we can. Learning how to write persuasively can also help you learn to sort out the messages you receive from others.

You have a better chance of winning over your readers if you:

▶ Start by summarizing a few important facts.

▶ State your own opinion or feelings.

▶ Use facts to support your opinion.

▶ Express what you want your audience to do or think in easy-to-understand language.

keep in mind

Persuasive writing can come to us as:
▶ *advertisements*
▶ *campaign speeches*
▶ *book reviews*
▶ *commercials*
▶ *newspaper editorials*

WRITING THAT COMPARES

Even when you are not aware of it, you are looking at things and *comparing* them. In your mind, you are noting how things you see are similar and different. It's a way to tell one thing from another. Writing that compares tells how two things are alike or different. You can compare two people, places, things, animals, or ideas.

Good writing that compares:

▶ introduces a clear main idea.

▶ gives similarities and differences, or advantages and disadvantages, of two things.

▶ gives details that help the reader "see" the comparisons.

▶ uses comparing words, such as *also, like, but,* and *in the same way.*

▶ organizes facts and ideas logically.

You can use writing that compares for many different purposes—book reports, news stories, science papers, and even travel guides!

EXPOSITORY WRITING

Suppose you were asked to write a report on crocodiles and alligators in the Florida Everglades. What kind of information would you need—and how would you find it?

Expository writing informs the reader. To make your report stronger, use description to help others "see" your ideas. Share information that your audience may not already know.

▶ Gather your facts from books, magazines, and the Internet.

▶ Make a plan! Organize facts and observations in an outline.

▶ Develop your main idea with vivid, unusual details.

▶ Write a clear beginning, interesting middle, and a strong ending.

PSST!

Add interest to your report with photographs, drawings, a chart or a graph.

STORY

What makes a story fun to read? What keeps you interested? A favorite character? A special setting? Surprising events? A good story *entertains* the audience. This means that a reader stays interested from the beginning to the end.

Map It Out!

These are the elements a writer uses to create a story:

▶ **characters** are the people in the story who carry out the action.

▶ **the plot** tells what happens in the story and what the characters do.

▶ **dialogue** is the conversation between characters that helps to make the story come to life.

▶ **setting** shows the story's time and place.

▶ **sequence of events** is the order of how things happen.

A story often tells about a problem, and how the characters solve it. Use your imagination! Your story will come to life with vivid descriptions, sensory images and original events.

keep in mind

Words like these can help you tell a story in correct sequence:
▶ first
▶ next
▶ then
▶ afterward
▶ later
▶ eventually
▶ finally

Arrange your thoughts in a logical order. You might describe your best friend from hat down to shoes or a freight train from engine to caboose.

PURPOSES
FOR WRITING

TO ENTERTAIN What will my audience enjoy? Entertain with silly song lyrics, a funny story, an animal adventure, a friendly letter.

TO INFORM People want to learn about things. They want to know *why* and *how*. They need information they can use to make decisions.

TO PERSUADE You want your readers to buy, to act, to join. You're looking for help or you want to make a change. Choose your words wisely and give reasons to support your requests.

TO REFLECT Writing down your thoughts and feelings helps you think about the world around you. Deciding to share your reflective writing can help others understand you better. Reflective writing can also help a writer to form questions and solve problems.

WRITER'S JOURNAL

Do you enjoy collecting commemorative stamps, dolls, or baseball cards? Whatever you collect, it's a real treasure to you. Writers collect ideas and memories, dreams and thoughts. They keep them in a special treasure chest called a *journal.* Writers who have been keeping a journal for a long time have learned that stashing things away little by little can produce a fortune of ideas. But where can YOU go when you need something to write about? It's time to start your own valuable writer's collection if you haven't already done it. Give it a try. Treasures await you!

Your journal does not have to be fancy. An ordinary notebook is great! Think of your journal or diary as a place, not a thing—a place where you can express the thoughts and feelings that are you.

You won't always have your journal with you. When you see or hear something you want to remember, write it on whatever is handy, like a used envelope. You can copy or tape it into your journal later.

Making It Your Own

Your journal does not need to look like anyone else's. Maybe the right thing for you is a book-like diary full of blank pages. You might enjoy using a binder where you can add, remove, and rearrange pages whenever you like. A file box of index cards can work the same way. You might even want to set up a journal folder on your computer.

Since a journal is a place to express your imagination, it might make sense to create your own notebook. Use paper and other art materials to assemble and decorate your own journal.

Logging In

Some writers use something called a *log*. A log is more a collection of facts and observations than of feelings. Travelers record places, dates, and mileage. Scientists make notes about experiments and research results. When might you use a log?

more **INFO**

Reflective writing and journals seem to go hand-in-hand. Review reflective writing on page 19.

Get in the habit of writing in your journal for at least a short time each day. The more you write, the more you'll find to write about.

LISTENING AND SPEAKING

PARTNERS

On the next few pages, you will be looking at what it takes to be an effective speaker and a good listener. Even while you are working on a writing project, there are chances to practice your listening and speaking skills. This is the perfect time to work with a partner.

Time to Listen

Ask your partner to read over your writing. Pay attention to what your partner says, and think about it. If you don't understand what your partner means, be sure to ask questions and discuss it. You may not agree with all the suggestions, but they will help you think about your work.

Take Turns

Be sure to take time to read your partner's work, too. Start by saying something positive. Then talk about parts that could be improved. If you don't understand part of your partner's writing, ask about it. Explaining it to you will help your partner write about it more clearly.

SMALL GROUPS

Listening to what others have to say will help you come up with new ideas of your own. When you have worked in a small group, how many of these strategies have you practiced?

▶ Only one person should speak at a time.

▶ Give everyone an equal chance to contribute.

▶ If you know you have made a lot of comments already, tell yourself that it is time for you to listen more.

▶ Be considerate of each other. Everybody's ideas are valuable.

▶ Some group members may not feel comfortable about speaking. Ask encouraging questions, and be kind with your words.

▶ You can disagree in an agreeable way. Arguments do not help the group. Try saying, "Here's why I disagree with that."

▶ When you speak, address your comments to everyone in the group. Try to make eye contact with each person.

▶ Ask questions when you don't understand what a group member has said or if you want to hear more. Then be sure to listen to the answer.

keep in mind

When you're not speaking, are you really listening? Listening takes energy. So "Listen Up!" and exercise your ears and your brain.

It's important for partners to speak to each other with positive words.

23

LARGE GROUPS

Can you think of times when you were part of a large audience listening to a speaker? Perhaps it was an assembly at your school. Maybe you have had a chance to be the speaker, too. How you speak to a large audience and how you listen both involve important communication skills.

keep in mind

Practice, practice, practice! Before you speak to a group, rehearse with a friend or a family member, or in front of a mirror. Your audience will know you are with them if you do not have to look at your notes all the time.

Giving and Getting Information

▶ A speaker who wants to inform should be sure to express the speech's main ideas along with details that tell more about those ideas.

▶ When you listen for information, try to organize what you hear. Ask yourself, "What new things am I learning about this topic?" and "What can I do with this new knowledge?"

When a Speaker Wants to Entertain

▶ Whether the speaker is portraying a famous character or describing an exciting vacation spot, an entertaining speech should be full of vivid words.

Persuasive Talk

▶ To persuade your audience, use reasons that make sense.

▶ Speeches to persuade are all around you. A TV commercial is really trying to persuade a large group, too—you and everyone else who is watching. Listen for arguments that are fair and honest. Can you tell the difference between fact and opinion? Don't get carried away by exciting language alone. It can mislead you.

INTERVIEWS

Interviews are valuable research tools when you explore topics during the Prewriting stage.

During an interview, you need to take turns being both speaker and listener. Here are some tips for both parts of the job.

When You Ask the Questions:

▶ Prepare for the interview. Think about the reason you are interviewing this person. Write down the questions you want to ask beforehand. Leave spaces in between to take notes.

▶ As you begin the interview, tell what your purpose is. You might say, "I'd like to find out how you choose the topics of your books."

▶ Bring your list of questions with you and use it.

▶ Be polite. Let the person finish talking before you ask the next question.

▶ Pay attention to the person you are talking with. Make eye contact whenever you ask a question.

When You Listen:

▶ Jot down the answers you are given, or at least a few key words that will help you remember what was said.

▶ Be an active listener. Your facial expression will tell whether you are really interested or not. When listening, try not to think about what your next question is going to be.

keep in mind

There are many good reasons for doing interviews. You may want information or stories about a person's experiences, or someone's opinions on a particular topic.

You don't have to just use the questions you bring to an interview. You may think of others when you hear some of the answers.

25

PRESENTING

Listening and speaking are skills that work together. Being a good listener can make you a better speaker. When giving a speech, a person often discusses different aspects of one topic. By listening, you gather detailed information that can help you to focus your questions. Careful listening also helps you to decide whether or not you agree with the speaker.

Points for Listeners

▶ Be a good audience member. Focus all your attention on the speaker.

▶ Take notes so that you can remember facts and details that make a strong impression.

▶ Use your notes to think of at least one question for the speaker. Preparing questions helps you focus on what is being presented.

Points for Speakers

▶ Rehearse and plan your presentation.

▶ Know how long you will be allowed to speak, and keep to the time limit.

▶ Be prepared for questions that you have not researched! Offer to find answers and to share them later.

VIEWING AND REPRESENTING

VIEWING

What can you learn by watching someone give a presentation? Watch the speaker closely. How do you think he or she feels about the topic? What clues do you have?

▶ Listen carefully. Make detailed notes of what you hear.

▶ What is the purpose of the talk?

▶ What part of the talk do you remember most? Why?

▶ When looking at a picture, chart, or video, jot down things that catch your eye.

REPRESENTING

Make a plan! How will you begin your talk? What do you want to say? What is the best way to say it? The people in your audience are an important part of your plan, so keep them in mind.

▶ Pictures, maps, or charts can help bring your ideas to life. Use them to get the audience more involved in your presentation.

▶ Use note cards to keep your presentation steps in order.

▶ *Rehearsing* is practice. Plan where and how to stand or sit, how to use your voice, and how to manage your materials.

PSST!

Rehearse! The better prepared you are, the more you will keep the audience's attention.

PART TWO

Study Skills & Language Skills

CONTENTS

STUDY SKILLS

DICTIONARY

Look it up! When you write, the **dictionary** is your source for spellings and meanings.

The dictionary is arranged in alphabetical order. Use the **guide words** to find the exact entry you need. You'll find a different pair of guide words at the top of each dictionary page. They stand for the first and last entries on that page.

Entry words are the words you look up. You can find them easily on the page. They are printed in darker type so they stand out. If you don't know the correct spelling of the word to start with, it may take you a little trial and error to find it.

For each entry word, you will see the word's meaning and the respelling, which helps you pronounce the word correctly. Some words have more than one meaning. The meanings are listed in numerical order. You will also find the part of speech and, in some dictionaries, the origin of each word.

A special type of dictionary called a **glossary** can be found in some of your schoolbooks. A glossary is usually several pages long, and it will list specialized or unfamiliar words used in the book. There is probably a glossary in the back of your science book, for example.

ATLAS

When you need to know the states in the South-east region of the United States or find the oceans that border Africa, you'll need a source that gives you "the big picture." An **atlas** can do it for you. It is a book of maps. Most large atlases start with a map of the entire world and the separate continents. Then maps of individual countries may be shown. In large atlases published in the United States and Canada, you will also find maps of each state and province, and maybe even certain large cities.

It may be easy to find a specific large geographical area you are looking for in an atlas. However, locate a city, river, or mountain range by using the **index** in the back of the atlas—an alphabetical list of all the places shown on the maps. Besides giving you a page number, it may also give a letter and number like G-7. This number will match the lines of latitude and longitude that crisscross the map and will help you track down a specific location.

CARD CATALOG

Believe it or not, there is a quick and easy way to find just the book you need amid the thousands or more in your library. Your library probably has either a **card catalog** or a **computer database** that allows each reader to search for books. It's much easier than "searching the stacks" of books on the shelves.

Filed in the drawers of the card catalog are cards for each book in the library. The drawers and the cards are arranged in alphabetical order. Fiction books have a **title card** and an **author card.** Nonfiction books also have a **subject card.** You can start your book search if you know at least the title, author, or subject of a book.

The information on each book's card includes a **call number.** It matches the label on the spine of the book. The numbers are based on the Dewey Decimal System. It is a way of assigning certain numbers to certain kinds of books. If you are confused about where to find a book on the shelf, ask the librarian for help. Soon you'll learn how to find books yourself using the numbers. It's like unlocking a secret code.

Perhaps your library uses a computer system instead of a card catalog. It works in much the same way. You need to type in the title, author, or subject of the book you are looking for. The computer then guides you through the screens to the call number you need.

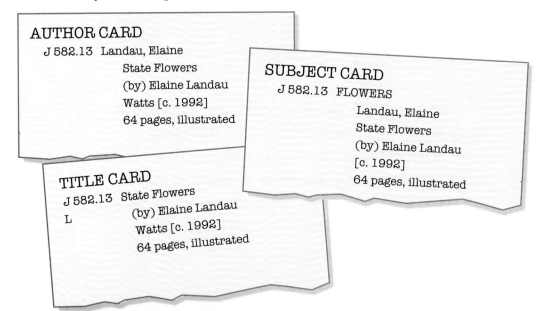

AUTHOR CARD
J 582.13 Landau, Elaine
        State Flowers
        (by) Elaine Landau
        Watts [c. 1992]
        64 pages, illustrated

SUBJECT CARD
J 582.13 FLOWERS
        Landau, Elaine
        State Flowers
        (by) Elaine Landau
        [c. 1992]
        64 pages, illustrated

TITLE CARD
J 582.13 State Flowers
L   (by) Elaine Landau
        Watts [c. 1992]
        64 pages, illustrated

ENCYCLOPEDIA

When you have a report to do, a good starting place is often an **encyclopedia**. The information about each topic is written in an **article**. Encyclopedia articles can be anywhere from several lines long to many pages.

If a certain article is very long, the encyclopedia divides it into parts. If you look up an article called "The Solar System," you might find different sections titled "The Sun" and "The Planets."

Encyclopedias can be found in the reference area of your library. There are also encyclopedias that you can use on the computer in the library or at home. There are some that contain only articles about certain subject areas, such as medicine or religion.

Encyclopedias include a number of books called **volumes**. The volumes, and the articles in them, are arranged alphabetically. If you are looking for information about the solar system, look in the volume for "S." Then use the **guide words** at the top of each page to find the exact article you need. The guide words tell you the first and last articles found on each page.

If you look in the last volume of most encyclopedias, you will find an **index** of the topics covered.

TELEPHONE DIRECTORY

A **telephone directory** is more than a list of phone numbers. The white pages of a phone book list the names, addresses, and phone numbers of individuals who live in a specific city or area. These pages are arranged in alphabetical order according to people's last names. There are **guide words** at the top of each page that give the first and last entries for that page. If you think that finding a phone number in the white pages is a lot like using the dictionary, you are right.

The yellow pages of a phone book are like an encyclopedia. The listings are arranged alphabetically by the kind of store, service, or business each one falls under. Many businesses include extra information about themselves in their listings. You might enjoy searching your telephone directory for names and information on local "Restaurants" or "Toy" or "Book" stores. What other kinds of listings might interest you?

Telephone directories give even more information. The pages at the beginning contain such things as emergency numbers, instructions on how to make long-distance and other types of phone calls, time zones, local maps, and useful information about community services.

CHARTS AND TABLES

Charts and tables are ways to present information visually. Charts can show a variety of information, but tables are usually used to give data in number form. Charts and tables are organized in rows and columns. The headings of the rows and columns name the categories of information.

With charts you can compare and contrast information easily. You might make a chart to list and compare the features of moths and butterflies. Your chart can list facts divided into categories called "How They Look" and "Their Life Cycle." If you need to decide whether to buy a new video game or a pair of skates, your chart can list reasons for and against each choice.

The table below displays the results of a school lunch survey. The numbers stand for the number of students in each grade who picked each food. How do the grade levels compare? Which food was the overall favorite?

FAVORITE SCHOOL LUNCHES			
	pizza	chicken nuggets	tacos
First graders	35	50	15
Second graders	42	18	40
Third graders	29	39	21
Fourth graders	32	20	41
Fifth graders	44	28	25
TOTALS	182	155	142

MAPS

We can use different maps to do different jobs for us. The maps we use the most often at school are called **political maps**. They help us find different places and the borders between them. A map of South America that shows all the countries and their capital cities is a political map.

A **physical map** of the same continent might still show those things, but it would also indicate how the land looked. You would get a more realistic idea of the Andes Mountains that run all along the western coast of the continent and the plains areas in other places.

See how many other kinds of maps you can find. There are road maps, product maps, population maps, and climate maps, for example.

On maps, you will see a **compass rose** that helps you find north, south, east, and west. There is usually a **key** listing the meanings of the symbols used on the map. A **distance scale** tells you how many miles or kilometers are represented by a certain unit of measure, usually an inch.

DIAGRAMS

Diagrams are pictures that show you the parts of different things. **Labels** are used to name the parts of the diagram. Diagrams can be a real help for understanding what things look like, how they are put together, and how they work. The way an electric circuit works, for example, can be explained with a diagram.

SCHEDULES

To keep your life organized, you might use a special kind of chart called a **schedule**. Schedules list the days and times of certain activities. Airplane flights and city buses run according to schedules. A calendar is a kind of schedule, too.

Saturday

9:00	Soccer Practice
12:00	Work on science project at Andy's house
3:00	Help rake leaves
5:00	Movies with Mike

GRAPHS

Allowance $10

Movies $6.50

Snacks $1.50

Arcade Games $2.00

A **graph** gives you information in a picture-like way. It allows you to compare different pieces of information, usually involving numbers. One type of graph is a **bar graph;** another is a **circle graph.**

This circle graph shows how Ben spends his weekly allowance.

37

DIRECTIONS AND LABELS

Have you read any good boxes lately? If you think about it, we do spend a lot of time reading packages and cans. Containers for food and other products give us a lot of information, but reading them is a little different than reading your favorite book.

Food **labels** are now required to list the nutritional value of the food inside the package. Look at two different packages of snack food. Which is better for you? It may be hard to decide. One is lower in sugar but higher in fat. How about an apple instead?

Directions for preparing food can be a cookbook recipe for making a cake from scratch or directions on a packaged cake mix. Both involve reading, gathering ingredients, and following a step-by-step process.

Other kinds of directions include instructions on how to get to your house: *Walk three blocks north of the Town Square. Turn left on Friendship Street.* Even things like planting seeds need directions.

Sunflowers

DIRECTIONS
SOW after the danger of frost has passed.
PLANT in rows 2 feet apart.
PLANT 1/8 inch deep.
COVER seeds.
THIN seedlings to 12 inches apart.

E-MAIL

Computers and other forms of technology are becoming part of our lives. If you use a computer you may be familiar with electronic mail, usually called e-mail. E-mail is a fast way of sending and receiving messages through the computer. You can send messages to a person or business. You can ask questions, conduct short interviews, or get up-to-the minute facts and information. Sometimes, classmates can work on group assignments together by using e-mail.

FORMS AND APPLICATIONS

By now, you are an expert at writing your name and probably your address and phone number. Many things we do require an **application form**—signing up for sports, applying for a library card, filling out a petition to run for Student Council. Many forms ask you to print your responses. However, the word *Signature* means you are expected to sign your name.

LIBRARY CARD APPLICATION FORM
MISTY SPRINGS DISTRICT LIBRARY

NAME James Chang
ADDRESS 256 West 12th St. S.W.
Central City, California 90583
PHONE 642-1234
DATE OF BIRTH 11-5-94
EMPLOYER OR SCHOOL Pacific Elementary
☑ I promise to abide by the rules of the Misty Springs District Library.

James Chang
(signature)

Another type of form that people often use is an **order form.** If you take orders for products you sell for your school or team, you already know about them. Just as with an application, you need to read and fill out an order form according to the directions. In addition, you will want to make sure your math is correct when you write down the amount you owe or need to collect.

LANGUAGE AND LITERARY SKILLS

PUNCTUATION GUIDE

End Punctuation

Use end punctuation at the end of a sentence.

A **period** ends a declarative sentence.

> Joe is my brother.

A **period** ends an imperative sentence.

> Turn right here. Please tell me a joke.

A **question mark** ends an interrogative sentence.

> How many apples do you have?

An **exclamation mark** ends an exclamatory sentence.

> Sandy rode her bicycle for five miles!

Periods

Use a **period** at the end of an abbreviation.

> Friday—Fri.   Road—Rd.   Mount—Mt.

Use **periods** in abbreviations for time.

> 5:25 P.M.   1:00 A.M.

Use **periods** after initials.

> J. McKenna   Carol W. Foster

Use a **period** after numerals and letters in outlines.

    I. Farm equipment
      A. Tractors
      B. Plows

Commas

Use a **comma** between the name of a city and a state in an address.

    New Orleans, Louisiana   Houston, TX

Use a **comma** before and after the name of a state or a country when it is used with a city in a sentence.

    I lived in Bakersfield, California, and Portland, Oregon, while I was growing up.

Use a **comma** between the day and year in a date.

    April 15, 2003

Use a **comma** before and after the year when it is used with both the month and the day in a sentence. Do not use a comma if only the month and year are given.

    I got my cat on February 12, 1998, for my tenth birthday.

    I got my cat in February 1998.

Use **commas** to separate three or more items in a series.

    Frank likes to eat carrots, peas, and beans.

Use a **comma** before *and, but,* and *or* when they join simple sentences to form a compound sentence.

    The flowers are fresh, and they smell very nice.

Use a **comma** after the greeting in a friendly letter and after the closing in all letters.

    Dear Sally,   Sincerely,

Use a **comma** to set off a direct quotation.

"I'm looking for guppies," Daniela said.

Use a **comma** to set off the words *yes* and *no* when they begin a sentence.

Yes, I have a pet.   No, my pet is not for sale.

Colons

Use a **colon** to separate the hour and the minute when you write the time of day.

I worked until 8:30 last night.

Use a **colon** after the greeting in a business letter.

Dear Sir or Madam:

Quotation Marks

Use **quotation marks** before and after a direct quotation, the exact words that a speaker says.

Mary commented, "The baby is getting sleepy."

Use a **comma** to separate a phrase such as *he said* from the quotation itself.

"I can't wait," Amos said, "to see you tonight."

Place a **period** inside closing quotation marks.

Her mom replied, "I'll meet you after school."

Place a **question mark** or an **exclamation mark** inside the quotation marks when it is part of the quotation.

Jennifer moaned, "Why can't you make it?"

Use **quotation marks** around the title of a short story, a song, a short poem, a magazine or newspaper article, and a chapter of a book.

Short Story: "Jack and the Beanstalk"
Song: "Old MacDonald Had a Farm"

Italics (Underlining)

Use **italics** or **underlining** to set off the title of a book, film, magazine, or newspaper.

<u>The Secret Garden</u>   *Highlights for Children*
Los Angeles Times

Apostrophes

Use an **apostrophe** and an *s* (*'s*) to form the possessive of a singular noun.

Susanne's folder   the building's lobby

Use an **apostrophe** and an *s* (*'s*) to form the possessive of a plural noun that does not end in s.

the men's softball game   women's tennis

Use an **apostrophe** alone to form the possessive of a plural noun that ends in *s*.

the girls' clubhouse   the employees' lunchroom

Use an **apostrophe** in a contraction to show where letters have been left out.

I + am = I'm   here + is = here's

Hyphens

Use a **hyphen** to show the division of a word at the end of a line. Divide the word between syllables.

I was hoping that the talent show would im-
press you.

Abbreviations

Most abbreviations begin with a capital letter and end with a period.

Mr.   Rd.   Feb.   Corp.

In informal writing and on envelopes, you may use U.S. Postal Service abbreviations for the names of states and the District of Columbia.

Alabama—AL	Maryland—MD	Oregon—OR
Alaska—AK	Massachusetts	Pennsylvania
Arizona—AZ	—MA	—PA
Arkansas—AR	Michigan—MI	Rhode Island
California—CA	Minnesota—MN	—RI
Colorado—CO	Mississippi—MS	South Carolina
Connecticut—CT	Missouri—MO	—SC
Delaware—DE	Montana—MT	South Dakota
District of	Nebraska—NE	—SD
Columbia—DC	Nevada—NV	Tennessee—TN
Florida—FL	New Hampshire	Texas—TX
Georgia—GA	—NH	Utah—UT
Hawaii—HI	New Jersey—NJ	Vermont—VT
Idaho—ID	New Mexico—NM	Virginia—VA
Illinois—IL	New York—NY	Washington
Indiana—IN	North Carolina	—WA
Iowa—IA	—NC	West Virginia
Kansas—KS	North Dakota	—WV
Kentucky—KY	—ND	Wisconsin—WI
Louisiana—LA	Ohio—OH	Wyoming—WY
Maine—ME	Oklahoma—OK	

In scientific writing, use abbreviations for units of measure. The abbreviation is the same for singular and plural units.

inch—in.   pounds—lb   kilometer—km   liter—l

CAPITALIZATION GUIDE

First Word in Sentences

Capitalize the first word of a sentence.

Cats have soft fur.

Capitalize the first word of a direct quotation. Do not capitalize the second part of an interrupted quotation unless it begins a new sentence.

The librarian said, "Please check the card catalog."

"I will," Sue replied, "when I have time."

Capitalize all words in a letter's greeting.

Dear Friends,

Capitalize the first word in the closing of a letter.

Sincerely yours,

Proper Nouns: Names and Titles

Capitalize the names of people and the initials that stand for their names.

Susan C. Ishing   S. C. Ishing

Capitalize titles of respect and abbreviations of titles when they come before the names of people.

Ms. Harmon   Major Nyson   Mr. Barnes   Dr. Lopez

Capitalize words that show family relationships when used as titles or as substitutes for a person's name.

First, Uncle Jim and Mother arrived.

Do not capitalize words that show family relationships when they are preceded by a possessive.

My father drove us to the station.

45

Capitalize the pronoun *I*.

> Will I need a sweater for our hike?

Proper Nouns: Names of Places

Capitalize cities, states, countries, and continents.

> San Diego   Oregon   Brazil   Antarctica

Capitalize the names of geographical features.

> Indian Ocean   Sonora Desert

Capitalize the names of sections of the country.

> the East   the Southwest

Do not capitalize words used just to show direction.

> We drove to the mountains west of our town.

Capitalize the names of streets and highways.

> Harwood Street   Highway 1

Capitalize the names of buildings and bridges.

> Empire State Building   Throgs Neck Bridge

Capitalize the names of stars and planets.

> Venus   North Star

Capitalize *Earth* when it refers to the planet. Do not capitalize *earth* when it is preceded by *the.* Do not capitalize *sun* or *moon*.

> From space, Earth appears green and blue.
> Dinosaurs roamed the earth.

Other Proper Nouns and Adjectives

Capitalize the names of schools, clubs, and businesses.

> Rolling Hills High School   Campfire Girls
> National Biscuit Company

Capitalize the names of historic events, periods of time, and documents.

Korean War   Ming Dynasty   Magna Carta

Capitalize days of the week, months of the year, and holidays. Do not capitalize the names of the seasons.

Tuesday   June   Memorial Day   summer

Capitalize abbreviations.

Carlton Smith, Jr.   Sun.   Mrs. Janet Burke

Capitalize the first word and all important words in the titles of books, plays, short stories, poems, films, articles, newspapers, magazines, TV series, chapters of books, and songs.

Book: *Two Bad Ants*   Play: *Hello, Dolly!*
Newspaper: *Newsday*   Magazine: *Time Out*
Short Story: "Goldilocks and the Three Bears"
Book Chapter: "The Giant Redwoods"
Song: "On Top of Old Smokey"

Capitalize the names of ethnic groups, nationalities, and languages.

Chinese   Australian   German

Capitalize the first word of each main topic and subtopic in an outline.

I. Team sports
   A. Ice hockey
   B. Soccer

USAGE GUIDE

Forming Noun Plurals

You can use this chart to spell plural nouns. Remember, some plural nouns have irregular spellings.

Singular Nouns	To Form Plural	Examples
most singular nouns	add *s*	girl dog hat girls dogs hats
nouns ending with *s, ss, x, z, ch, sh*	add *es*	box watch kiss boxes watches kisses
nouns ending with a consonant and *y*	change the *y* to *i* and add *es*	hobby city sky hobbies cities skies
some irregular nouns	change their spelling	tooth foot man teeth feet men
a few irregular nouns	keep the same spelling	moose deer trout moose deer trout

Adjective Forms

You can use this chart when you need help with comparative and superlative adjective forms. Remember, some adjectives are irregular. They do not form their comparative or superlative forms in the usual way.

Adjective	Compares Two	Compares More Than Two
small	smaller	smallest
thin	thinner	thinnest
lengthy	lengthier	lengthiest
tiny	tinier	tiniest
active	less active	least active
likable	more likable	most likable

Verb Forms

Irregular verbs do not add *ed* to form the past or past participle.

Verb	Past	Past Participle
be	was, were	(have, has, or had) been
do	did	(have, has, or had) done
go	went	(have, has, or had) gone
begin	began	(have, has, or had) begun
come	came	(have, has, or had) come
run	ran	(have, has, or had) run
sing	sang	(have, has, or had) sung
swim	swam	(have, has, or had) swum
drive	drove	(have, has, or had) driven
eat	ate	(have, has, or had) eaten
give	gave	(have, has, or had) given
ride	rode	(have, has, or had) ridden
take	took	(have, has, or had) taken
write	wrote	(have, has, or had) written
draw	drew	(have, has, or had) drawn
grow	grew	(have, has, or had) grown
fly	flew	(have, has, or had) flown
see	saw	(have, has, or had) seen
throw	threw	(have, has, or had) thrown
wear	wore	(have, has, or had) worn
bring	brought	(have, has, or had) brought
make	made	(have, has, or had) made

WRITING TERMS

audience	the reader or readers for whom something is written
brainstorming	a way to focus a writing topic by listing any thoughts that come to mind about the topic
charting	a way to organize and classify ideas and information by gathering them under different headings
checklist	a list of items, such as tasks or topic details, that can be used as an organizer and as a reference source. *See also* **listing.**
chronological order	the arrangement of events in the order in which they occur in time. *See also* **time order.**
clustering	a way to explore ideas by gathering details related to the specific writing topic
compare	to explain how two or more things are alike
conference	a meeting between the writer and a partner or a teacher, or in a group, to ask and answer questions about the writing in progress, with the purpose of improving it
contrast	to explain how two or more things are different
description	a piece of writing that creates a clear and vivid picture of a person, place, or thing
detail sentences	sentences that tell more about the main idea of a paragraph
diagram	a visual or graphic presentation of information; often used to organize information during prewriting. A Venn diagram is particularly useful for comparing and contrasting.
drafting	the act of capturing ideas on paper; a stage in the process of writing during which the writer gets his or her basic ideas down on paper

elaboration	a writing strategy in which facts, examples, reasons, images, and other details are added to a piece of writing in order to give the topic fuller treatment
entertaining writing	writing, often humorous or suspenseful, that amuses, intrigues, diverts, or engages the reader for the particular purpose of entertainment
explanation	writing that presents the facts about a subject in a clear and logical way
expository writing	writing that presents information to a reader in a clear, accurate, complete, and coherent way
freewriting	a way to generate ideas by simply writing continuously for a specified time, without stopping to elaborate or to correct errors
instructions	an explanation or set of directions for how to do something. The steps in a set of instructions are arranged in a logical way, so that other people can repeat the activity.
letter	a way to communicate informally or formally with someone in writing. A friendly letter has six parts and is personal in nature. A business letter has six parts and is written to an audience often unknown to the writer.
listing	a way to organize your thoughts by writing them down and putting them in order—possibly by numbering them
logical order	an arrangement of ideas in an order that makes sense and is easy for the reader to follow
outline	a way to organize topic-related ideas in the order in which they will be discussed—especially useful in organizing a research report

paragraph	a section of a written work, consisting of one or more sentences on a single subject or idea and beginning on a new and indented line
personal narrative	writing in which the writer tells about something that has happened in his or her life
persuasive writing	writing that encourages an audience to share the writer's beliefs, opinions, or point of view
prewriting	the stage in the writing process in which the writer chooses an audience, a purpose, and topic, explores ideas, researches and organizes material before drafting
prewriting strategies	particular ways of gathering, exploring, planning, and organizing ideas before writing a first draft. *See entries for some prewriting strategies*: brainstorming, charting, clustering, freewriting, listing, outline, story chart, *and* time line.
proofread	to review writing in order to correct errors in punctuation, capitalization, spelling, and grammar
publish	to share written work with an audience—for example, by reading it aloud, contributing it to a school paper, or posting it on a bulletin board
purpose	the writer's reason for writing—for example, to explain, to entertain, or to persuade
reflective writing	writing in which the writer's personal thoughts, ideas, or feelings become an important part of the form. That form can be a poem, a story, or an essay, for example.
report	writing that provides information about a specific subject. A book review is a report that gives information about a book the writer has read. A research report summarizes information from many sources about a subject.
revise	to improve a draft by adding or taking out information, combining and reordering sentences, elaborating, or changing word choice according to the purpose and audience

sensory details	in a description, the details that appeal to the reader's five senses—sight, hearing, touch, taste, and smell
story chart	a way to gather ideas and details under headings important for the writing of a story
style	a writer's use of language and sentence structure to create a particular tone
summary	an account that tells the most important ideas of what has been read or observed by the writer
supporting details	facts, examples, or sensory details that give more information about the main idea of a paragraph
time line	a way to organize events in chronological order
time order	the arrangement of events in a composition according to when they occur in time—also called chronological order. Some time-order words are *first*, *next*, *then*, and *last*.
tone	the feeling or attitude a writer expresses toward the subject of a composition through his or her particular style of writing. For example, a writer's tone may be formal, informal, humorous, or critical.
topic sentence	a sentence that states the main idea of an informative, explanatory, or persuasive paragraph
transition words	words or phrases that may help writers to compare and contrast, such as *on one hand* and *on the other hand*; also, words that link sentences in a narrative, such as *finally* and *in the meantime*
voice	the quality of a piece of writing that makes it distinctively the writer's own
writing process	the stages involved in writing, which usually include prewriting, drafting, revising, proofreading, and publishing

GRAMMAR TERMS

action verb a word that expresses action

  She *raced* to the car.

adjective a word that modifies, or describes, a noun or pronoun

  That is a *sour* apple.

adjective phrase a prepositional phrase that modifies, or describes, a noun or pronoun

  The dress *of red silk* is gorgeous.

adverb a word that modifies a verb, an adjective, or another adverb

  She played *well.*

adverb phrase a prepositional phrase that modifies, or describes, a verb, an adjective, or an adverb

  The man stands *near the door.*

antecedent (referent) a word or group of words to which a pronoun refers

  Stan is a fabulous writer, but *he* needs a good editor.

article a special adjective—*a, an,* or *the*

  The horse took *an* apple from *a* trainer.

common noun a noun that names any person, place, or thing

  The *airplane* landed.

complete predicate all the words that tell what the subject of a sentence does or is

  Jerry *grew tomatoes and lettuce.*

complete subject all the words that tell whom or what the sentence is about

  Sally Jacobs is my best friend.

compound sentence a sentence that contains two sentences joined by a comma and the word *and, or,* or *but*

  I sang a song, *and* she played the piano.

conjunction	a word that joins other words or groups of words in a sentence
	The friends shopped *and* ate dinner.
direct object	a noun or pronoun that receives the action of the verb
	Jane gave a *speech* to the class.
helping verb	a verb that helps the main verb to express action
	Sarah *was* running fast.
indirect object	a noun or pronoun that answers the question *to whom? for whom? to what?* or *for what?* after an action verb
	Bill gave *me* a rose.
linking verb	a verb that connects the subject of a sentence to a noun or an adjective in the predicate
	Joe *is* a secretary.
noun	a word that names a person, place, or thing
	The *dog* chewed on a *bone* in the *kitchen.*
object of a preposition	a noun or a pronoun that follows the preposition in a prepositional phrase
	I bought a vase in the *shop.*
object pronoun	a pronoun used as an object of the preposition, a direct object, or an indirect object
	Please give the book to *me.*
possessive noun	a noun that shows ownership
	The *girl's* father came to the play.
possessive pronoun	a pronoun that shows ownership
	Our dog is a collie.

predicate adjective	an adjective that follows a linking verb and describes the subject The boy is *smart*.
predicate noun	a noun that follows a linking verb and describes the subject Carla was the *president*.
preposition	a word that relates a noun or pronoun to another word in the sentence She gave me a box *of* cookies.
prepositional phrase	a group of words that begins with a preposition and ends with a noun or pronoun The glass *on the counter* is mine.
pronoun	a word that takes the place of one or more nouns and the words that go with the nouns *He* lent *me* a quarter.
proper adjective	an adjective formed from a proper noun She bought an *African* basket.
proper noun	a noun that names a particular person, place, or thing The *Pacific Ocean* is immense.
run-on sentence	two or more sentences that have been joined together incorrectly I bought a cake yesterday it was chocolate.
sentence	a group of words that expresses a complete thought John and David wrote a letter to their aunt.
sentence fragment	a group of words that does not express a complete thought Wrote a letter to their aunt.
subject pronoun	a pronoun that is used as the subject of a sentence *He* likes baseball very much.

LITERARY TERMS

alliteration	the repetition of the same first letter or initial consonant sound in a series of words Glen gave Gilda a goofy gift.
autobiography	the story of a person's life written by that person
biography	the story of a real person's life written by someone else
character sketch	a long description of a character that tries to present a thorough and vivid portrait of the character
characters	the people (or animals) who participate in the action of a story or play
concrete poem	a poem whose shape suggests the subject of the poem
dialogue	the conversations the characters have in a story or a play
fiction	written work that tells about imaginary characters and events
figurative language	words used in unusual rather than in exact or expected ways, frequently in poetry. *Simile* and *metaphor* are two common forms of figurative language.
free verse	a poem that sounds like ordinary speech and has no regular rhythm or rhyme
haiku	a poem of three lines and usually seventeen syllables in which the poet frequently reflects on life or nature
idiom	an expression with a special meaning different from the literal meanings of its individual words—for example, "Time flies."
imagery	the use of word pictures—images—to make a description more vivid through especially precise or colorful language
limerick	an English verse form consisting of five lines that rhyme *a a b b a*. The third and fourth lines have two stresses, and the other lines have three stresses.

lyrics	the words of a song
metaphor	a figure of speech in which a comparison is made without using the word *like* or *as*
	The field was a green blanket.
meter	the regular pattern of beats in a poem
nonfiction	written work that deals with real situations, people, or events
onomatopoeia	words that imitate actual sounds
	The kitten's *meow* was very cute.
personifi‑cation	a description in which human qualities are given to something that is not human
	The leaves chased each other across the playground.
plot	the action or sequence of events in a story, novel, play, or narrative poem
repetition	the use of the same word, phrase, or sound more than once, for emphasis or effect, in a piece of writing
rhyme	the repetition of syllables that sound alike, especially at the ends of lines of poetry
	The wrinkled sea beneath him crawls; He watches from his mountain walls, And like a thunderbolt he falls.
rhythm	a pattern of stressed and unstressed syllables, like a regular musical beat, especially in a poem or song
	And hand in hand, on the edge of the sand, They danced by the light of the moon.
setting	the time and place in which the events of a story occur
simile	a figure of speech in which a comparison is made using the word *like* or *as*
	The kite soared like a bird.

stanza	a group of lines in a poem that forms a complete unit, like a paragraph in a piece of prose writing
story	writing that has a sequence of events, or plot. The people in the story, or the characters, move the action of the story along. The setting is where and when the story takes place.
tall tale	a story in which the characters are larger than life and able to perform extraordinary feats. Exaggeration is used in a tall tale.
tanka	a poem of five lines and usually 31 syllables (5, 7, 5, 7, 7), which frequently expresses the poet's reflections on a topic from life or nature
theme	the main idea or meaning of a complete piece of writing
tone	the total effect of the language, word choice, and sentence structure used by a writer to express a certain feeling or attitude toward the subject

SPELLING AND VOCABULARY

As a writer, you go through a long process to get your work the way you want it. You want it to be your best. When you proofread, then, be sure to check that all words are spelled correctly. Not only is it helpful to your readers, but it allows you to know that your work will be understood. A misspelled word can sometimes even change your meaning.

The tips and rules in this section will help with some spelling patterns and problems. Remember to use your dictionary or ask for help whenever you are unsure how to spell or pronounce a word.

SPELLING STRATEGIES

Helping Yourself

It is possible to spell some words by saying them aloud to yourself and writing down the letters for the sounds you hear. It will help to say each syllable separately. Then look at the word you wrote. You can often tell when a word doesn't look right. At least the letters you do have will give you a headstart when you head for the dictionary.

It might be a good idea to add a section to your journal for words that are challenges for you to spell.

Below are some spelling rules. They will help you to spell words that follow similar patterns. But beware of exceptions!

s and es Endings

▶ With many words, you can just add *s* to form the plural:

coat/coats   can/cans   parrot/parrots

▶ For words that end in *ch, s, ss, sh, x,* or *z,* add *es:*

patch/patches   bus/buses   glass/glasses

brush/brushes   mix/mixes   buzz/buzzes

▶ If a noun ends with a single *f,* change the *f* to *v* and add *es* to make it plural:

shelf/shelves   loaf/loaves   calf/calves

BUT, watch for "rule breakers" like these:

roof/roofs   chief/chiefs

es, ed, ing, er, and est Endings

▶ For words ending with a consonant followed by *y,* change the *y* to *i* before adding an ending that does not begin with *i:*

pony/ponies   try/tried   happy/happiest

▶ When a word ends with a vowel followed by *y,* you usually just add the ending:

spray/spraying   enjoy/enjoyed

▶ In most cases, if a one-syllable word ends with one vowel and one consonant, double the consonant before adding an ending that begins with a vowel:

stop/stopped   plan/planning   win/winner

▶ When a word ends with a silent *e*, drop the *e* before adding an ending that begins with a vowel:

pale/paler   nice/nicest   hope/hoping

ie and *ei* Words

▶ Many words have a long-e sound spelled *ie*. But when the long e follows a *c*, it is spelled *ei*:

piece   belief   chief   yield
BUT: receive   ceiling   receipt

▶ For most words with a long-*a* sound, the correct spelling is *ei*:

eight   sleigh   reign

▶ Remember this rhyme:

"*I* before *e*, except after *c*,
Or when sounded like |ā|,
As in *neighbor* and *weigh*."

It usually works!

But there are some *weird* exceptions:

either   seize   weird

VOCABULARY BUILDING

Building with Prefixes

▶ A **prefix** is a word part that can be added to the beginning of a word.

▶ The word to which a prefix is added is called the **base word** or **root word.**

Adding a prefix produces a word with a new meaning, sometimes one that is the exact opposite of the base word.

▶ The prefixes *un* and *dis* mean *not* or *the opposite of:*

unfinished   dishonest

▶ The prefix *re* means *again* or *back:*

retie   retell   replace

Think about how prefixes change meanings:

prefix	meaning	base word	new word
mis	bad or wrong	pronounce	mispronounce
im, in	not, without	possible	impossible
trans	across	Altantic	transatlantic
non	not	fiction	nonfiction
sub	under, below	freezing	subfreezing
tri	having three	angle	triangle

Spelling with Prefixes

When a prefix is added, the spelling of the base word usually does not change:

correct/incorrect   view/preview

Building with Suffixes

▶ A **suffix** is a word part that can be added to the end of a word.

▶ The word to which a suffix is added is called the **base word** or **root word.**

suffix	meaning	base word	new word
ful	full of	thank	thankful
less	without	pain	painless
ly, ily	in the manner of	quiet	quietly
able	capable of being	return	returnable

Spelling with Suffixes

▶ If a base word ends with a silent *e*, you usually drop the *e* before a suffix that begins with a vowel:

love/lovable   operate/operator

▶ If a base word ends with a silent *e*, you usually just add a suffix that begins with a consonant.

care/careless   pave/pavement

HOMOPHONES

Words that sound the same but have different meanings and spellings are called **homophones.** Check the dictionary when you are unsure of which spelling to use. This list contains several homophones. How many others can you think of? You may want to write them in your journal.

sea/see	real/reel	through/threw
to/too/two	hours/ours	pair/pear/pare
so/sew/sow	forth/fourth	principal/principle

TRICKY SPELLINGS

Many words are exceptions to the rules of spelling. When you are unsure of a word, use this list or your dictionary. The more you use tricky words, the sooner you will remember how to spell them.

address	color	interest	recognize	than
afraid	cough	interrupt	recommend	their
again	decide	island	remember	there
against	different	its	rhyme	they
although	disappear	it's	rhythm	they're
answer	early	know	said	though
beautiful	enough	knowledge	says	thought
because	especially	language	schedule	through
been	except	library	school	tired
believe	favorite	lightning	scissors	together
bicycle	February	many	separate	tomorrow
bought	forty	minute	similar	toward
breakfast	fourth	misspell	sincerely	trouble
breathe	friend	money	some	truly
brought	front	necessary	special	until
build	great	neighbor	straight	very
busy	guess	ninth	successful	weather
buy	half	none	suppose	we're
caught	happiness	often	sure	where
certain	heard	once	surprise	whether
children	height	people	taught	women
close	hour	probably	tear	would
clothes	instead	receive	terrible	written

PART THREE

Writing Models

CONTENTS

WRITING MODELS

PERSONAL NARRATIVE

Mrs. Schultz is the best friend our school could have. She used to be our school secretary. She still was when I was in kindergarten. Then Mrs. Schultz retired from her job. But she sure didn't retire from being a valuable helper.

When we were learning to read in first grade, she would come in and help our teacher. She would take a few of us and read us a brand new library book full of interesting pictures. Whenever she came to an unusual or funny-sounding word, she would stop and teach us how to read it.

Everybody thinks of Mrs. Schultz's funny earrings whenever you mention her name. One Third Grade Field Day, Mrs. Schultz arrived with a tiny baseball hanging from one ear and a miniature baseball bat from the other.

I wonder what Mrs. Schultz has up her sleeve, or on her ears, for this year.

Just Me

I've had a good summer, but the day I liked best happened two weeks ago. Mom said that she and I were going to have a special day all to ourselves. When you're the oldest, it seems like that never happens. In fact, Mom gets so busy with my brother and sister sometimes that I think she's just glad I can take care of myself.

Well, that day, Dad took care of everything at home. Mom and I took a bus all the way downtown. When we got off, we were in front of the tallest store. We took an escalator up and up for eight floors.

On the eighth floor, we ate at a beautiful restaurant. I only ordered a hamburger and fries, but it came on a fancy white plate with gold around the edge. I drank out of a goblet. It looked like a little bowl with a stem growing out of it. While we ate, Mom and I really talked. She asked me how things were going at school. She listened when I told her about the new games we were doing in gym and about the things that were bothering me.

The rest of the day was fun, too. We looked around a great toy store for a whole hour, and we bought ice cream from a cart on the sidewalk. Mom said we'll have to take trips like that more often and that she misses having time with just me. Me, too!

EXPLANATORY WRITING

HOW TO DRESS LIKE A FOOTBALL FAN

If you're like me, you probably have a favorite team. Here's how to be the best-dressed fan for your team.

1. Put on a shirt that is the same color as your team's uniforms. You may even have a shirt with the team's name and symbol on it.

2. If you're going to an outdoor game, you might need to add a sweatshirt. Be sure it's the same color as your T-shirt.

3. Wear sweat pants that have your team's name written down one leg.

4. Put on a cap that has the team's design on it.

5. Get a big pin that says, "Go Team!" Pin it on your shirt.

6. For really cold games, take along a team blanket, and use a team cushion for sitting on those hard bleachers.

7. Go to the game and have a good time whether your team wins or loses. And don't forget your ticket!

Acid and Eggs

The experiment I did for my science project involved vinegar and an egg. I used vinegar because it is high in acid, which is a chemical compound. Many foods we eat are high in acid. Vinegar itself is found in pickles and salad dressings. Some other foods that are high in acid are oranges, tomatoes, pineapple, and cherries.

Why did I use an egg for my project? Finish reading my experiment and see if you can discover the reason.

1. First, I placed the egg in a clean glass jar. The jar was big enough for the egg not to get stuck when I put it in or took it out.
2. Then I poured vinegar into the jar, totally covering the egg.
3. I waited for three days.
4. After three days, I took the egg out of the vinegar. The hard eggshell was gone. Only the skin from under the shell was holding the raw egg together.

The reason I used an egg is that it contains calcium like our bones and teeth do. I learned that the acid in the vinegar had a chemical reaction with the calcium in the eggshell and dissolved it. Acids in the foods we eat can do the same thing to our teeth. We can help protect our teeth from cavities by brushing soon after we eat.

PERSUASIVE WRITING

May 2, 2001

To the Editor:

I have noticed a problem at our town playground that needs to be solved. Whenever I go there to play with my friends, there are a lot of big kids there, too. Sometimes we can't play basketball because they won't let us. Also, a lot of older girls sit on the swings and talk, so the younger kids can't use them. The playground was built for kids our age and younger.

I have a few ideas that might help. Maybe the school newspaper could print a story about the playground and what is happening there. Also, parents could ask their older children to leave the playground for the younger kids. If the teenagers don't have other places to go, the town should think about providing places for them.

I hope the kids and the town can work together to find a solution for this problem.

Sincerely,

William Barnett

William Barnett

Voter News

My name is Tasha Banks, and I am in Mr. Bernardi's fourth grade class. I want to be your Student Council President for next year. I think I have good ideas and the experience needed for the job.

I have been my class's Student Council representative this year and last year. I think I did a good job of listening at all the meetings and reporting back to my class. I also try to ask the people in my class what they think Student Council should do about certain things. That is where I got the idea to ask for more clubs for students after school. This year Drama Club got started, and next year Art Club will be added.

I have some new ideas, too. I think students in our school might like to be on a committee that welcomes special visitors to our building. If I am elected, I will work with the other members of Student Council to see if they think this is a good idea, too.

These are some of the reasons I think I would be a good Student Council President. I hope you will vote for me in the election next week. Thank you.

WRITING THAT COMPARES

Plants in Sand and Water

The aloe is a desert plant that thrives in sandy soil. It lives for a long time without water, sometimes for many years. It is a succulent plant. This means that it stores water in thick leaves and draws very slowly on the supply. The inside of the leaves is like a thick gel. It can be applied to the skin to treat sunburn or scratches.

However, the lotus plant has very different needs. Unlike the aloe, which has a long-lasting water supply in its leaves, it is very dependent on a watery environment. It always grows in a body of water, such as a lake or pond. While the aloe has comparatively short roots in dry soil, the lotus has very long roots attached to the rich, muddy soil at the bottom of its pond. It sends a long shoot to the surface of the water, where a beautiful flower opens up. The lotus is considered a special ingredient in Chinese cooking.

The aloe and the lotus are good examples of how different plants require very different environments.

City Kid, Country Kid

My family lives in Chicago, and I love everything about it. There are a lot of fun things to do here. We have a great art museum, and many smaller art galleries. Our basketball team, the Bulls, is one of the best teams in the country. And my dad takes us to lots of games! The city is a big, noisy, exciting place to live. Chicagoans walk, talk, and do everything pretty fast. I wouldn't live anywhere else.

However, I also like to visit the country. My cousin Jen lives on a farm in Spencer, Indiana. I spend my summer vacations there. When I go to Jen's, it takes me a few days to slow down. Unlike Chicago, Spencer has no tall buildings, no busy streets full of people and cars. It has quiet country roads and fields of tall grass. On Friday nights, instead of going to sports games, I play pinochle with my cousins on their back porch. During the day, I get to ride my uncle's old horse, Bart. That's very different from riding the El trains in Chicago!

I like the excitement of the city, and the fresh air of the country. Both places are good to experience for different reasons.

EXPOSITORY WRITING

Lewis Carroll

Lewis Carroll was an English writer who lived from 1832 to 1898. He wrote many things, but he is most famous for two children's books called *Alice's Adventures in Wonderland* and *Through the Looking Glass*.

Lewis Carroll was the oldest of 11 children. When he was young, he liked to do magic tricks and perform marionette shows for his family. He would even publish his own newspapers and put his original poems in them. He graduated from college and became a math teacher.

Lewis Carroll was the author's pen name—the name he used when he wrote. His real name was Charles Lutwidge Dodgson. He created his pen name from the Latin words for his first and middle names. He invented another word you may have heard—*chortle*. It is a combination of the words *chuckle* and *snort*. You can find *chortle* in Carroll's nonsense poem "Jabberwocky."

Lewis Carroll may have lived a long time ago, but we certainly still enjoy his work today.

Two Rivers

The Nile and the Amazon are the longest rivers in the world. The Nile River in Africa is 4,145 miles long, and the Amazon River in South America is 4,000 miles long. They are similar in length but still very different.

The Nile flows north through different land regions, from tropical forest to savannas to high grass to desert. Savannas are flat, open plains. The yearly rainfall along the Nile varies from 1 inch in desert areas to 50 inches in the southern part. Some animals found in the Nile are fish, snakes, turtles, crocodiles, and lizards.

The Amazon flows east, mainly through the world's largest rain forest. The rain forest is called the *selvas*. The annual rainfall is about 79 inches. The Amazon and the land all around it have more than 2 million species of insects, 2,000 species of fish, and 600 different mammals.

Even where the Nile flows through the desert, people have been able to live and farm near it. When it used to flood every year, the water left good soil on the land. Floods are controlled now, but irrigation brings water to farmland. Almost all the people of Egypt live close to the river.

In South America, however, the Amazon flows through the rain forest, and very few people have lived near it until now. More people are developing the land now, and scientists are worried about the effects of that development on the rain-forest environment.

The Mysterious Mr. Foster

When Mrs. Jackson pushed aside her curtain one morning, her trash cans were still full, but there was an empty box on the ground. The box had been full of old wire and pipes the night before.

The next week, Mr. Novak looked out his window just in time to see someone carrying away a shopping bag. The cover was off one of his trash cans.

Neighbor after neighbor started to realize that things were disappearing from their trash.

About two weeks later, everyone found envelopes stuck in their front doors. Inside were invitations to a party in Mr. Foster's garage on Saturday afternoon. Nobody knew Mr. Foster very well, but everyone was curious about his party and eager to go.

On Saturday, all the neighbors were treated to snacks and lemonade. Mr. Foster was friendly in his quiet way. All that seemed strange was the blanket covering the workbench.

After a little while, Mr. Foster asked for quiet and said, "I'm a shy person who doesn't visit with other people too often. But you've all been such nice neighbors that I wanted to say thanks."

With that, he pulled the blanket from the workbench. Sitting there were several animal-like creations. "I'd like each of you to have one of my creations," he announced. "I made them by recycling things you threw away." The mystery was solved.

Camping

It was a clear, starry night at camp. The girls and leaders in Sharon's troop had hiked to a spot by the lake. They made a fire and sang songs. The evening ended with scary stories. Little did Sharon know she soon would be in one herself!

The girls started back to the "campsite." They would be sleeping in a huge old house in the woods. The house must have been beautiful at one time, but now it was run-down.

When the group reached the house, they were tired and cold. But when the leaders tried to unlock the door, it would not open. Finally, they realized that it could only be opened from the inside.

Sharon found a window that was unlocked. Soon the grownups were able to push it open. The window was very narrow—too narrow for anyone but Sharon to get through. She didn't want to admit how nervous she was as they helped her through the window and into the house. Her heart was pounding, and she felt lost.

The only light was a flashlight shining in from outside. Finally, Sharon found the door, almost by accident. She unlatched the lock. Everyone piled in, relieved and ready for bed. Then Sharon lay awake in her sleeping bag for a long time. For the next camping trip, she wanted a tent!

Illustration
Part 1: Teresa Cox 4–5, 6 (strip), 12 (strip), 18 (strip), 20 (strip), 22 (strip); BB&K (tech art) 6, 7, 10, 11; Margaret Shinnick 7a, 7b, 7c, 7d, 16a, 16b, 22, 24, 26, 27; Peter Spacek 10, 11a, 11b, 12a, 12b, 16; Dorothea Sierra 20, 21; Michael Sloan 18a, 18b, 19b, 19c. **Part 2:** Mary Thelen 28–29, 30 (strip), 40 (strip), 60 (strip); Dorothea Sierra 31, 33a, 33b, 36; BB&K (tech art) 32, 34, 37, 39; Michael Sloan 35; Peter Spacek 38; Jennifer Beck Harris 49, 54, 62, 64.
Part 3: Leah Palmer Preiss 66–67, 68 (strip); Margaret Shinnick 70, 76, 77; Michael Sloan 72, 73.

Design and Production by BB&K Design Inc.